THE WONDERS OF SEEDS

D1457806

THE WONDERS
OF SEEDS

ALFRED STEFFERUD

Illustrated by Shirley Briggs

New York

HARCOURT, BRACE AND COMPANY

LIBRARY OF CONGRESS CATALOG CARD NUMBER: 56-6921

PRINTED IN THE UNITED STATES OF AMERICA

21988

CONTENTS

THE WONDERS OF SEEDS

1 : SEEDS THAT SLEPT
A THOUSAND YEARS

Long ago a strange thing happened to a lake in faraway South Manchuria. It suddenly disappeared. It never came back. Probably nobody would know it ever existed if it had not left behind some mysterious seeds buried deep in the mud of the lakebed.

This lake was about two miles long and two miles wide. Elm trees, poplars, and willows grew thick and tall along its shores and on the high hills farther back. The water was blue like the sky. But you could not have seen all of the water's surface, because a great mass of water lilies grew in the lake. The lilies had pink flowers as big across as your two

3

hands. Each flower was like a shiny star and had many pointed petals. The leaves were two or three feet across. Some of the leaves floated on the water, like giant saucers and green shields. Some leaves grew on stalks six feet above the water, like parasols.

After the petals of the flowers had dropped off in the fall, a sort of pod could be seen in the middle of each flower. It looked like a cup or the bottom half of a top that has been cut in two. Inside the pod were about a dozen dark-brown seeds, each nearly one-half inch long. They were like big acorns or small pecan nuts. Their shells were very hard, but children liked to break them open and eat the soft, creamy kernels inside.

The children and their parents in the nearby village of Pulantien called the plants sacred lilies, or lotus. Very likely they thought the lake was sacred, too, and would last forever.

But the lovely lake near Pulantien did not last forever. No one knows why or how the lake vanished or how long ago.

Maybe some great movement like an earthquake or the eruption of a volcano deep inside the earth raised up the floor of the valley, so that the water of the lake drained away and changed the course

4

of the river that flowed into and out of it. Or maybe some very heavy rains came suddenly and made the outlet of the lake so large that all the water rushed out.

At any rate, the trees and the lilies and other plants—mosses, reeds, and rushes, which also grow in water—were thrown together into a thick mass. In time they rotted in the mud and became the spongy, black-brown material that we call peat. We get peat from bogs and sometimes we put it on our gardens and lawns to make the soil more porous.

Then strong winds blew from the west, carrying dust from far-off Gobi Desert. The lakebed, plants, and peat were covered with a layer of dust up to five feet deep. Nothing could be seen of what once was blue water and green trees and the fragrant lotus flowers.

Buried also amid the mass of plants and peat were the seeds of the lotus in their top-like pods. The tough coverings, almost as hard as stone, kept the seeds safe and sound through the heat of many summers, the cold of many winters, and the rains of many springs.

The seeds slept in the dirt and peat for a long time, keeping within themselves a spark of life until the time might come when they could sprout and produce new plants.

Sometimes farmers would uncover some of the seeds when they plowed their fields in the old lakebed before they planted their wheat, millet, and sorghum. Sometimes they would uncover seeds when they dug some of the peat for fuel to heat their houses. They would eat the seeds, which still tasted good after all those years. The farmers and the people in Pulantien village never thought the seeds would some day excite the interest of scientists all over the world. But that was what happened not many years ago.

Scientists learned about the seeds from U. Liu, who owned the land where the lake had been and who had been a teacher of the Chinese language in schools in Tokyo. As a boy on the farm near Pulantien he had eaten the seeds. All his life he had wondered about them. What could they be? How had they gotten there? Finally he gave some of the seeds to Ichiro Ohga, a friend who was a Japanese botanist in Tokyo.

"How old are the seeds?" Ichiro Ohga asked. "What are they? Will they grow?"

U. Liu could give no exact answer.

His ancestors had migrated to the Pulantien basin

6

about two hundred years earlier, he said, and four generations of them had farmed the land. So the lake might have disappeared two centuries ago. Or, he added, there might be a link between the age of the seeds and the fact that Mongolian soldiers had settled on the land as farmers about five hundred years before.

What would you do if you had a puzzle like this to solve—a puzzle you felt sure had a lot to do with a problem that scientists have been studying for a long time?

Ichiro Ohga did what you would have done. He went to U. Liu's estate to look for clues there.

He found two clues. One clue was the size of the willow and poplar trees that were growing in the old lakebed. He knew that willows and poplars do not grow in water. Therefore these must have begun to grow after the lake had dried up. From the thickness of their trunks, Dr. Ohga estimated that the willows were one hundred twenty years old and the poplars one hundred fifty-six years old.

The other clue had to do with the Pulantien River, which now flowed near the basin where the lake had been. All these years the river had steadily carried away some of the soft soil of the basin so

7

that the river ran deeper and deeper below the level of the lakebed.

Mr. Liu pointed to a large rock that rose thirty inches out of the water.

"I could not see that rock in the river thirty years ago," he said. "So I judge the river is washing away the soil at the rate of one inch a year."

That was the yardstick Ichiro Ohga needed. He measured the banks of the river and found they were about four hundred inches high.

"Therefore," he told himself, "it has taken the river four hundred years to carve out its high banks through the peat and mud. The lake might have disappeared and the river might have changed its course four hundred years ago."

So he determined that the seeds might be anywhere from one hundred twenty to four hundred years old. He could not be sure, of course. A scientist has to know exactly. He cannot guess at facts, and he cannot suppose that something is true.

So he went back to his laboratory in Tokyo and made other tests to see if he could learn more about the seeds. He got some of them to sprout—which means they were viable, or still living. He read about experiments of other botanists and felt certain then that his seeds were the oldest viable seeds that any scientist had ever found.

He tested two hundred seeds. All were viable. He asked himself, "Why did they not sprout before in the old lakebed?"

He kept some of them in water for eight months. They did not change at all. He filed a hole through the hard shells of some of them. They took up

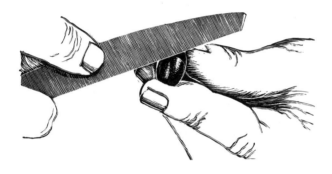

water and became swollen and were ready to sprout. He treated some of them with different kinds of gases. He learned that in order to sprout they needed oxygen, which is in water and air. The shells had kept the gases and water out during the long years the seeds had been buried. He soaked some of the kernels in a strong acid for a whole day. The acid was so strong that a drop of it would burn his hand if he was not careful with it, but it did not kill the seeds. That showed how tough they were.

He learned a great deal about those seeds and all seeds from his experiments. Some seeds stay viable better when they are buried in soil. They need oxygen or air to sprout. Seeds take longer to sprout if they have hard, tough coverings, or seed coats, as we call them. That is one of the ways Nature uses to make sure that plants will not disappear from the earth even though lakes and rivers and trees and the surface of the earth and other things might change or vanish.

Ichiro Ohga gave some of the seeds to scientists in other countries. A few went to two men who knew a great deal about the forms of plants and animals that existed long ago. Those men decided that the seeds might have been buried fifty thousand years ago at a time when the earth's crust was uplifted in that part of Manchuria as it was in many other parts of the world.

Other scientists doubted that the seeds could be that old, even though they knew that the hard seed coats could keep the seeds in good shape until conditions were exactly right for them to grow. The essence of science is proof, and proof that would convince the scientists was lacking.

Then came another test, with a new tool of science. It is called the radiocarbon 14 test. It is based on studies made by Dr. W. F. Libby, a scientist at the University of Chicago. He learned that radioactive carbon is formed in the atmosphere far above the earth when strong rays from outer space strike nitrogen, a gas that is a part of all living matter. Some of the carbon reaches the earth, and living plants and animals take in some of it from the air and their food and water. As the tiny particles in it break up and give off rays, the radioactive carbon disappears at a very slow and steady rate from the tissues of the plants and animals after they die or stop growing. This rate of disappearance can be measured. Therefore we can learn how long ago plants lived by measuring the amount of the radioactive carbon that remains in them. Dr. Libby used the test on the lotus seeds. He determined that very likely they were one thousand forty years old, although they might be two hundred ten years older or younger than that.

That is nothing like fifty thousand years, but nevertheless it is wonderful when one remembers that a seed is a living thing.

And so the mystery was unraveled, step by step. Just as detectives do when they seek the answer to some puzzling question, the scientists brought to bear on the mystery of the seeds what they knew of many branches of learning.

One more question remained. The seeds had sprouted in the laboratory. They had grown to the flowering stage. Would they grow into full-size plants under ordinary conditions?

One day two of the seeds arrived at the office of Horace V. Wester, a scientist in the National Park Service, in Washington. With great excitement he opened the little package in which they came. He felt that he was at the beginning of a great scientific adventure.

At once he started to prepare the seeds for sprouting. He filed through one side of their flinty seed coats so that water could enter. He then soaked the seeds in water for fifteen minutes. By then the inner seed coats had burst, showing that they were taking up the water. Then he put the two seeds under moist cotton in a covered glass dish.

All this, of course, is different from the ways used by Nature to get seeds ready for sprouting. Sometimes the hard, thick seed coats are rubbed, cracked, and worn thin when wind or water carries them over sand and rocks. Some seeds may rot, and so water can enter the coverings. Animals and insects sometimes bite holes in the seed coats, or animals eat seeds and partly digest them. Nature helps the lotus seeds to sprout by letting them float on a stream or the coverings wear thin as they roll over gravel, sand, and rocks.

A period of anxious waiting followed for Mr. Wester. One day—no sign of life. Two days—the seeds were just the same. Three days—still no change. Four days. Five days. It was still too soon to expect any sign of life, but when Mr. Wester inspected his precious seeds on the fifth day he noticed that on one of them there was a tiny stem. The seed was sprouting! Two days later the other seed started to sprout.

As carefully as he would hold a baby, Mr. Wester planted the seedlings—the baby plants—in soil that he had sterilized with steam (to kill any weed seeds and harmful bacteria that might be in it) and had enriched with rotted cow manure. He put them in rather large pots. He put the pots in a tank of water in a greenhouse. That was as close as he could come to the seeds' original home in the lake near Pulantien.

The little plants seemed to like their new home. They grew so fast that in a month they had to be moved to larger pots.

But then came a period of disappointment and worry. The seedlings seemed to be dying. They stopped growing. Their leaves turned yellow and sickly. What had happened? Would all this work and study turn out to be in vain? They were transplanted to wooden boxes. The boxes were placed in a sunny outdoor pool in the hope that the sick plants would perk up. There they spent the first winter.

There was great excitement the next April among the people who worked with Mr. Wester. The lotus plants were growing again—and growing fast! What had happened when the leaves turned yellow was that the plants were in the resting period that all young lotus plants go through.

Now Horace Wester had another time of waiting. If all went well, he expected the plants to
blossom a year later, because three years is the
usual time it takes the lotus to flower after its seeds
sprout.

He did not have to wait that long, however. One
day in June he discovered that one of the plants had
stalks about seven inches long. There were flower
buds on the stalks. Two weeks later the other plant
also had buds. In four days the first pink flower

appeared. It was nearly seven inches across. A bud on the other plant opened about a week later. Its flower was a little lighter pink than the first one. A study of the parts of the flowers showed the plant to be a variety of the East Indian lotus. Its scientific name is *Nelumbo nucifera*. It grows wild in China, Japan, the Philippines, India, and Australia.

You can see the plants that grew from the seed Mr. Wester nursed so carefully if you visit the Kenilworth Aquatic Gardens in Washington, D. C. When you see them, remember this: They came from seeds about a thousand years old—the oldest living seeds ever discovered.

And now perhaps you are asking, "What is the good of knowing how old seeds can be?"

We were interested in the age of the lotus seeds because it gave us a new scientific fact about the world we live in. It helped in the study of seeds— how to preserve them, how long to keep them, how then to make them grow. This is an important practical matter in that farmers, gardeners, and others who plant or sell seed have to be sure that their seed will sprout. State and federal departments of agriculture carry on tests all the time to make certain that seed that is sold will grow well.

For example, some soybeans only six weeks old may not be able to sprout, but other soybeans have been good after ten years, depending on the conditions in which they have been kept. Wheat generally loses its ability to sprout after ten years, but some wheat that was carefully dried and kept in a sealed jar lived thirty-two years.

Some scientists once tested one hundred kinds of seeds that had been kept buried in the ground thirty-nine years at the old experiment station in Arlington, Virginia, where the Pentagon Building now stands. They found that thirty-six of the seeds— of tobacco, jimson weed, morning-glory, and pokeweed—were still alive.

At East Lansing, Michigan, sixty kinds of weed seeds were put away in moist sand in jars in 1879. Seventy years later two kinds were found to be still alive.

Many seeds had been stored for one hundred fifty years in a dry place in the British Museum in London. A bomb hit the museum in the war. It caused water to soak into the materials in which the seeds were kept and so gave them the moisture they needed in order to sprout. But of all those seeds only two kinds sprouted. One was seed of the mimosa tree. The other was the lotus.

2 : HOW SEEDS ARE MADE

You already know a great many seeds.

You have seen the oval, brown seeds inside apples. You come across white seeds in the oranges you sometimes have for breakfast. You have found many black, flat seeds in watermelons. You have eaten peanuts, beans, and peas. You have had walnuts and pecans in candies and cookies. Some of you have planted seeds of nasturtiums, morning-glories, and marigolds in your gardens. You may have noticed seeds of hollyhocks, hollies, and many other plants in gardens and parks and along roadsides in summer, fall, and winter. Maybe you have had to take "stickers" off your clothes when you have come back from a walk in a country field or woods. Maybe you have seen seeds of dandelions, milkweed, or maple trees carried around by the wind.

If you have looked at any of those seeds, you know that seeds of different plants are unlike in size, color, shape, numbers, and other ways. Some seeds are big. Some are small.

Coconuts, the seeds of coco palms, are among the biggest seeds. An even bigger one is the coconut of another kind of palm tree that grows on islands in the Indian Ocean. It may weigh as much as forty pounds.

Some seeds are so small they are like dust or powder. One kind of orchid has seeds so tiny that eight million of them weigh about an ounce. One single flower of this orchid can produce nearly four million seeds.

The reason orchids have so many tiny seeds is that orchids can grow only when soil, light, and moisture are exactly right for them, and seedlings of stronger plants can easily crowd out the small orchids. Therefore Nature increases the chances that orchids will continue to grow by insuring many seeds so small that they can be easily blown by wind to the most suitable places. The coco palm can sprout quite easily without much waste of seeds because it contains much stored food for use by the tiny plant as it starts to grow. Therefore it has only a few, large seeds.

The seeds of most plants that do not have too great a struggle to grow are neither very large nor very small. The average size of all seeds is about that of a kernel of rice or wheat.

Many of the most widespread kinds of .plants bear large numbers of seeds or else have special ways by which their seeds are carried far and wide.

Seeds are of many colors. Some corn kernels are white and yellow. You may have seen other corn that has blue, black, red, or purple kernels. Seeds of the castor bean are mottled, like the markings of some beetles. But most seeds are grayish or brown or some dull color. The color is due to pigments in the seed coats. Nature has a purpose or reason for nearly everything she does, but as far as we know she has no particular reason for coloring seeds one way or another.

Seeds have many different shapes. Some, like the pea, are round. The bean is oval. Grass seed is long. Melon and cucumber seeds are flat. Milkweed seeds are tufted. How the seed is placed in the fruit, how the seed is spread, and the shapes of the flower part that produces the seed determine the shapes of the seeds. In pea pods, for example, the peas, which are round seeds, are flattened if they are packed close together.

Seeds are alike in four ways, no matter what their color, size, shape, or number may be.

1. Seeds (except those of pine trees and related trees and shrubs) are formed in the flowers of plants. About 250,000 species of plants produce seeds.

2. Every seed, no matter how small, has in it a tiny plant, which may sprout—if we give it air, warmth, and water—and grow into a plant like the plant that made it.

3. Every living seed has some food in it for the tiny plant as it begins to grow.

4. Nearly all seeds have a covering that protects them. Sometimes the covering is so hard that you have to break it open with a hammer or a nutcracker. Some coverings are not hard, but tough, like plastic or cellophane.

You can easily make some experiments yourself to demonstrate these points.

First get some seeds. That should not be hard. Very likely you will find some dry peas or uncooked beans in your kitchen. They will do very nicely. If you cannot find them, peanuts or seeds of oranges and grapefruit will do.

Now take them apart. You can cut them with a knife or just pull off the outside covering and separate the parts with your fingers. That can be done easily if you soften them in water. First you will notice the one or two coverings which are the seed coats. Inside you will find two halves of the seed. Nestling inside them is the tiny plant. It is called the embryo. One meaning of the word *embryo* is *beginning*.

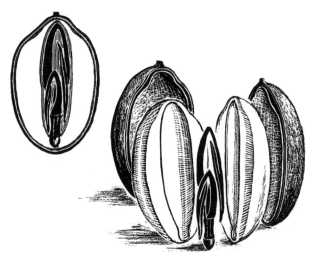

And here is another experiment. Buy at a seed store a packet of radish seeds—or, if you cannot get them, get some nasturtium or cucumber seeds. Place a few of them, about an inch apart, on a sheet of wet blotting paper in a saucer. On top put another piece of wet blotter. Put them in a warm place, and do not let the blotters dry out. The seeds will sprout in a few days. As you do not intend to plant them, it will be interesting to take one of the seeds every day and pull it apart to see how the coverings split open and how the parts of the seed begin to grow.

Another suggestion: In spring, look for seeds in your grapefruit that are beginning to sprout in the fruit itself.

Now, if somebody should ask you what a seed is, you will be able to answer. You might say that a seed is the thing from which a plant grows. You would be right. Or you might want to be more exact, and say a seed is a unit which has a tiny plant, food supplies, and protecting seed coats, and by which seed plants spread. Maybe you have heard the word *seed* used in other ways that have to do with the beginning of something. We speak of the *seed* of an idea, and mean the beginning or kernel of a thought. A farmer *seeds* a field with corn— his first step in growing a crop. *Seed* even is used sometimes to mean children, for children carry on the lives of their parents. All this shows how important we think seeds are.

Now you will want to know what makes a seed.

We begin with the flowers. Up to now you may have thought of flowers only as something beautiful —something to enjoy in bouquets or in gardens. They are much more than that. The real purpose of the flower is to form seeds.

Like seeds, flowers differ in their size, color, form, and parts. Duckweeds, which grow in ponds the world over, have flowers so small you can hardly see them. Rafflesias, which grow in the dense forests of Malaya, have flowers up to four feet across. The petals of some flowers look like leaves. Some flowers have spurs or tubes on the petals. If you have a chance to do so, compare the flower of the pea and the flower of the corn, which you may never have thought of as a flower—the bunch of "leaves" or husks from which the "silk" extends and the little "branches" at the very top of the corn plant itself.

Like seeds, flowers are alike in purpose and in the way their basic parts are put together.

Usually a flower has four main parts.

The outermost part is the calyx (*kay*-licks). It is the outer covering of the blossom. Often it is green and looks like a small leaf.

Just inside the calyx is the corolla (koh-*rohl*-la). This is what we often think of as the "flower"—the

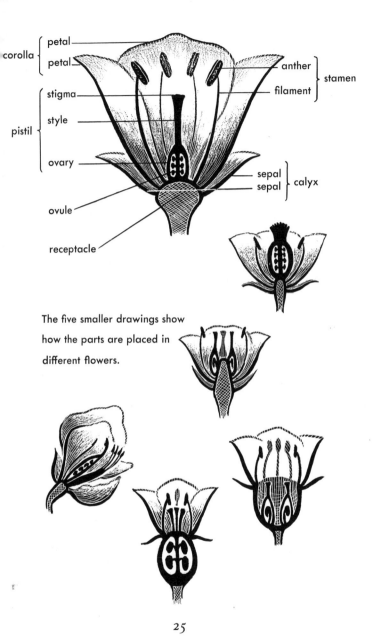

corolla { petal
         petal

pistil { stigma
         style
         ovary

ovule

receptacle

anther } stamen
filament

sepal } calyx
sepal

The five smaller drawings show
how the parts are placed in
different flowers.

21988

petals, which may be yellow, pink, blue, red, white, purple, or another color. The calyx and the corolla are actually the "leaves" of the flower. They cover the bud and protect the parts that produce the seeds.

The stamens (*stay*-mens) and the pistils (*piss*-tills) are the most important parts. Without them there could be no seed.

The stamens usually have a stalk and at the top a little case, which is filled with a powdery, dustlike matter which we call pollen (*pahl*-len).

The pollen is the life-giving spark. One grain of pollen may be so tiny that you can see it only under a microscope. The pollen of the forget-me-not is so small that six thousand grains measure only an inch. The pollen of the pumpkin is much larger than that—but even that is so small that one hundred twenty-six pollen grains measure an inch. You

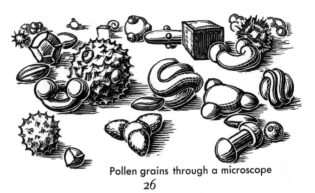

Pollen grains through a microscope

can see a mass of yellow pollen, but perhaps not the single grains, on a flower like a tiger lily. When you touch the stamens, the pollen comes off on your fingers.

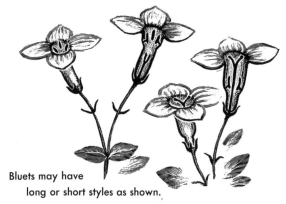

Bluets may have long or short styles as shown.

The pistils, one or more in the center of the flower, are the parts which grow into fruits and in which the seeds are formed. The top of the pistil is sticky or has many branches on a stalk. It holds the pollen grains which may touch it.

There are two special words, which we use over and over again. One of the words is pollination (pahl-lin-*nay*-shun), which means the movement of the pollen grains from the top of the stamen to the top of the pistil of the same or a different flower. The other word is fertilization (fur-tih-lih-*zay*-shun). It takes place when a tiny tube from a pollen grain unites with the tiny beginning seed inside the pistil, causing the seed and embryo to develop.

In some plants the stamens and pistils are close together, and the pollen has only a little way to go to reach the pistil. In other plants, Nature has made it hard or impossible for the pollen of one flower to fertilize the pistils in the same flower. The pollen has to come from another flower of the same kind. Then the pollen might be carried by the wind.

Strong winds sometimes carry the pollen from pine trees to other pines as much as four hundred miles away. In the fall, some people have "hay fever," which is caused by the great amounts of ragweed pollen carried in the air. It is said that a single ragweed plant can shed eight billion pollen grains in five hours. A tassel of corn, composed of many pollen-bearing flowers, may produce up to fifty million pollen grains. Pollination by wind usually occurs with such plants as the grasses, sage, ragweed, oaks, and walnuts, which have small, ordinary flowers that do not attract insects. Their blossoms have large amounts of light and powdery pollen that is easily blown, and feathery branched tops of pistils, to which the pollen can easily stick.

Many kinds of plants, especially those with bright,

fragrant flowers, are pollinated by insects, such as bees, wasps, butterflies, and moths. Hummingbirds, snails, and other living things also carry the pollen of one flower to the pistil of the same flower or the pistils of other flowers. Very likely there is something about the flower that attracts the creature— color, perfume, or a sweet, sugary nectar. In insect-pollinated plants, the top of the pistil is usually sticky.

We have seen bees busily visiting one flower after another in search of the nectar, which is food to them. In fact, we often think of bees and flowers as being closely connected—as, indeed, they are. The bee helps the flower and the flower helps the bee. And here is a remarkable thing: If a bee visits, say, a rose first, it will generally continue to visit only roses for a while, thus spreading the pollen from rose to rose and not from a rose to a morning-glory, where the rose pollen would do no good. By spreading the pollen, the bee helps make sure that more seeds will form, and then, in time, more flowers, which the bee needs, will grow.

On its legs the bee has a special basket in which to carry pollen. It also has special brushes on the legs that it uses to push the pollen that sticks to its body into the basket.

The transfer of pollen from one blossom to another blossom we call cross-pollination. The transfer of pollen from the stamen of one blossom to the tip of the pistil of the same blossom we call self-pollination.

Nature seems to prefer cross-pollination, and goes to great lengths to make sure that many kinds of plants are cross-pollinated. Here are a few examples: In the geranium flower, the tips of the pistils ripen before the stamens, so that the pollen will not fertilize pistils of the same flower but must be carried to other and older blossoms with pistils at the right stage to receive it. In the figwort the process is just the opposite—the stamens are ready before the pistils. A young flower of a salvia has curved and hinged stamens, so placed that a bee has to press against them when it enters the flower. The stamen then turns and dusts the bee with pollen and at the same time closes the way to the pistil. The pistil in an older salvia flower hangs down farther, so that when the bee enters it, the pistil gets the pollen from the other blossom. The primrose has flowers of two types. In one type, the pistils are long and the stamens are short. In the other type, the stamens are long and the pistils are short. That

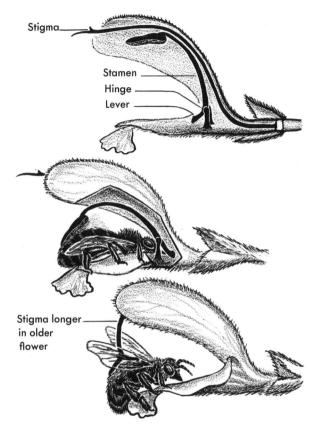

Stigma

Stamen
Hinge
Lever

Stigma longer
in older
flower

·makes it harder for the pollen to reach the pistil
of the same flower.

People who grow fruit, vegetables, flowers, and
other plants apply what they know about pollination in order to get better crops. For example, some
kinds of apple trees must have the pollen from other

kinds in order to set fruit. An orchard that has only Spitzenburg apples in it would yield few apples; there would have to be others like Baldwin or Jonathan apple trees to produce pollen for the Spitzenburgs. Pear orchards need to have trees of different varieties. Tomato plants grown in greenhouses do not have many tomatoes unless the plants are shaken when the stamens are shedding pollen or the pollen is collected and blown over the plants. The reason is that there is little wind and few insects in a greenhouse to carry the pollen around.

After pollination and fertilization, the seeds form. The inner seed coat often is thin and delicate. The outer one usually is hard, so as to protect the inside parts. They may be almost waterproof. Some can be soaked for a time in acids, alcohol, or the digestive juices of animals' bodies without being harmed. Sometimes the outer coat has a tuft of long hairs, as in the milkweed. Some seed coats are covered with cottony hairs, as in the cotton plant. Some may be extended into a wing, as in the trumpet-creeper.

In some seeds the stored food is a separate part, called the endosperm (*en*-doh-sperm), surrounding the embryo. In other seeds the larger embryo has absorbed and contains the stored food, and there is no endosperm.

The embryo, or tiny plant, is the all-important part of the seed. It usually consists of one or two seed-leaves or cotyledons (kotty-*lee*-dons); a stalk, which later grows into the root; and a bud, which becomes the main stem and leaves of the plant. Pines and related plants have several seed-leaves, instead of one or two.

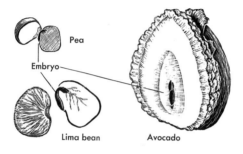

Pea

Embryo

Lima bean   Avocado

In making the embryo, all parts of the plant reach the goal of their existence. The function of the flower is to produce the embryo. The function of the fruit is to protect the embryo. The function of the seed is to feed the embryo and sometimes to carry it to another place. It is the beginning of life, and a step in the fulfillment of Nature's great law: Be fruitful and multiply.

And so seeds are formed. They are ready to grow. Some of them do so quickly if the soil and warmth are right for them. But many other kinds of seeds must wait a while before they sprout. They have to "rest" or "sleep" for a time, which we call a dormant period or dormancy. The word *dormant* means sleeping. Dormancy, the resting stage, is very important in the life of the plant. It is important also in man's use of plants, like wheat and corn, as crops for food. If seeds of tender plants would sprout at once, the winter cold would kill them all. Their seeds, then, are the way in which they go through the winter. Or, seeds that sprouted at once in late spring when they had enough rain might die during the dry spell that often comes in summer. So the seeds sleep until early the next spring when they have a better chance to get well started before dry summer weather comes.

Another thing: If all seeds of all the plants that we call weeds would sprout at one time they could all be killed off entirely by plowing fields just as the weeds were coming up. We might like to get rid of weeds in that easy way and save all the work of weeding our lawns, gardens, fields, and flower beds. But the point is that we disagree about what a weed is. To us, a weed might be any plant that is in a place where we do not want it. Dandelions are beautiful, but we do not like to have them in our lawns or flower beds. To Nature, though, all plants are important and must go on living.

34

3 : THE SEED SPROUTS

Ask your mother for four empty peanut butter jars or jelly glasses and some dry peas. If she asks what you want them for, say that, like any scientist, you want to test for yourself some statements that you read in a book.

Mark the jars A, B, C, and D. Put some cotton in the bottom of each jar and about a dozen peas on top of the cotton. Put no water in jar A. Cover the peas in jar B with water. Put just enough water in C and D to wet the cotton but not enough to cover the peas. Put jar D in a cold place, perhaps the refrigerator. Put the other jars in a warm place, such as a sunny window sill near a radiator. Cover all the jars with the cover they had or with saucers so that little water is lost by evaporation from the jars. Leave them alone for a week or two.

You will discover that the peas in jar A have not changed at all. Why?

The peas in jars B and C, in which you put different amounts of water, have made some growth.

In B the peas started to grow but stopped growing in a little while. Why?

In C the peas have kept on growing. Why?

The peas in D, which also had as much water as C, did not grow. Why?

If you can answer the *why?* each time, you know the three things seeds need in order to sprout: Warmth, which the peas in jar D did not have; air, which the peas in jar B did not have, because they were covered by the water; and water, which the peas in jar A did not have. Only the peas in jar C had all three—the right amount of water, air, and warmth.

Water, air, and warmth. You would think that it would not be hard for seeds to have all three. But only a small fraction of the vast number of seeds that are produced each year really get them at the right time. Many or perhaps most seeds are eaten by animals. Even if a seed should reach the right place many things can happen to keep a seed from sprouting.

The ground where a seed falls or is carried may be so hard it cannot get water, so cold that the seed is not warm enough, or so filled with water that it has no air. The seed may be in a place where grass or other plants already growing there take all the water. Or the place may be rocky, or sandy, or too hot. Some seeds, as we have seen, can rest for a long time, waiting for the right conditions. Some cannot. That is why some plants produce so many seeds—if one seed out of a million reaches the right place at the right time, that may be enough to keep that kind of plant alive from year to year.

Now let us see what happens when the conditions are right for a seed to grow into a plant. The tiny units of life in the embryo, called cells, divide again and again. The parts of the embryo get bigger and bigger and soon become stems, roots, and leaves. The sprouting of the seed, the change from seed to seedling, is called germination (jer-mih-*nay*-shun).

This growth is a time of great activity. It takes only a few days, but the changes are too small to follow with the human eye—just as it is hard to see the hour hand on your watch move. You would realize how exciting germination is if you could see it in a movie, in which a single picture is taken every five minutes so that the whole film of the growing seed and seedling could be run off in three minutes or so.

Then you would see that germination has three steps. First, the seed swells as it takes up water. Second, the seed coats soften and break as the embryo grows. Third, a part of the embryo pushes through the seed coats and lengthens to form the root and the stem.

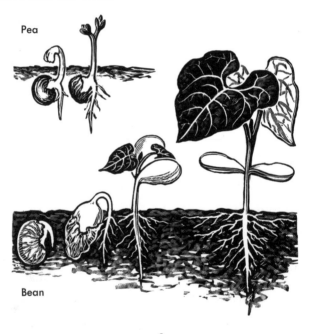

Water is needed for several reasons in the first step. To begin with, it dissolves the food stored in the seed so that the parts of the seed can use it as they grow.

In a fresh seed, the food is a moist, rich jelly that is packed around the embryo. As the seed ripens, the jelly dries and hardens into a form that will keep for a long time—up to a thousand years, as in the lotus seeds from the lake in Manchuria. When the seed is sown and takes up moisture again, the food material turns once more into a watery jelly that nourishes the root and stem until they can take care of themselves. You can see this for yourself in a kernel of corn. When you eat corn on the cob in the early fall, the fresh corn is soft and sweet. Later in the fall the corn ripens and the soft kernels harden and dry into starch, so that the corn may be kept a long time. Those ripe yellow ears are fed to animals, or the kernels are ground to make meal for corn muffins and many other things. If the dry corn is planted in spring, it soaks up water. The starch then changes back to sugar, a sweet sap that the embryo feeds on as it sprouts. The seed needs water to start these chemical changes.

Some seeds take up a great deal of water. The corn and wheat kernels absorb about half their weight of water, and the garden pea can take up its own weight of water.

The seed needs water also to soften the seed coat so the seed can breathe. When we breathe, we take into our lungs the oxygen that is in air and we breathe out the carbon dioxide that is formed in the processes of living. Much the same thing happens in seeds and plants, but because they do not have lungs, we use the word *respiration* to describe it. Seeds need a great deal of oxygen in sprouting. Seeds of only a few kinds of plants, like rice and cattails, will sprout well under water where the amount of oxygen is much lower than the amount of oxygen in the air. Many seeds will not germinate if they are deep in the ground, perhaps because they do not get the oxygen they need. You remember reading in the first chapter about the lotus seeds that lay so long in the deep layer of peat, where they got no air.

We said the sprouting of seed has three steps. We have just read about the first step, in which the seed takes in some water, swells as it feels the warmth, and stretches itself after its sleep.

Now comes the second step. Water is important here, too, for it softens the seed coats, so that the embryo can break through them more easily. A tiny stalk of the embryo gets longer and longer until it breaks through the coat of the seed.

Germination of corn

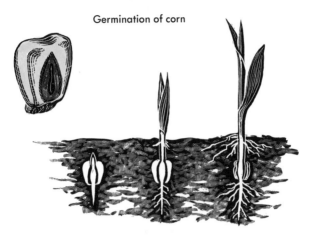

How can the small, weak stalk break through the seed coat of a cherry or walnut or lotus, for example, which you can hardly break with a hammer? That is possible because the water may have softened the coverings, as we have seen. In many seeds the absorption of water causes a great pressure, which breaks or cracks the coatings. You can see the result of this pressure if you fill a tumbler with dry beans, pour as much water as you can in the tumbler, and cover it with a saucer or a piece of glass. Soon you will see the beans swell so much as they absorb the water that they lift the cover off the tumbler. Or maybe you have seen how your mother cooks rice. She puts about a cupful of rice and the water in a rather large pan. If she puts the rice in a small pan it would swell so much as the water boils that it would lift the cover and go over the stove and floor!

For some seeds it may be necessary to file or scratch the coverings so as to make a hole to let the water get into the seed through the hard seed coat. Then the swelling seed does the rest.

There is a third possibility, which is a wonderful device of Nature. Some of the hard seed coverings grow in two halves (as in the walnut), and when they are wet they split along a line that Nature makes weaker than the rest of the shell just for this purpose. In some seeds, as in the coconut, there are special places, like "doors," that are weaker than the rest of the covering and that the stem of the embryo can force open.

In the third stage of sprouting the first part of the embryo to push out generally is the root. In grasses, such as corn, the root and stem both have protective sheaths over the growing tips, which emerge at two places.

The end of the stalk that first comes out of the seed turns down into the earth. The root forms on it. It is a strange thing, but no matter how the seed is put in the ground the root tip goes down toward the moisture in the soil.

Soon after the root has started to form, the bud of the embryo gets longer and grows into the main stem, which turns upward toward the light. The stem carries above the ground the seed-leaves and seed coats, as well as the first tiny true leaves formed in the bud within the seed. As the seed-leaves get bigger, they throw off the seed coats that protected them up to now.

In a bean seedling, you can see the two seed-leaves, each nearly half the size of the seed, rising up from the ground and spreading apart. But in some seedlings, such as corn, the seed-leaves and seed coats remain in the ground. The part of the embryo above the seed-leaves grows into the stem and leaves, while the part below the seed-leaves grows into the root. Thus stem and root are distinct from the beginning, and one does not fork to form the other. The short part between the two is called the hypocotyl (high-po-*cott*-ill).

New, bright-green leaves, which are called true leaves, begin to form and make food for the tiny plant. The food they make is sugar, and they use water, air, sunlight, and the green stuff in their leaves, called chlorophyll, to make it. Up to that time, the food for the tiny seedling has come from the sugar in the seed-leaves or the endosperm. All this time, the root keeps on growing downward and also to the sides, forming root hairs or tubes through which it takes from the soil the water and minerals the growing plant needs.

And so we have the baby plant. It can take care of itself (unless, of course, you step on it, or your dog digs it up, or it does not get the sun, warmth, and water it needs) and will grow into a full-size plant so that it also can produce seeds.

4 : SEEDS IN PACKAGES

Summer and its lovely flowers have gone. Fall and its lovely fruits and berries have come.

The flowers have nectar in them and bright colors to tempt bees, butterflies, hummingbirds, and other creatures to visit them and help in their pollination and fertilization.

The fruits and berries may be bright, too, and often sweet. You know the grapes—purple, white, and red. You may know the golden firethorn, the orange persimmon, the red barberry, the white snowberry, and the brown acorn. They and many like them may stay on the bushes and vines or trees until the leaves have fallen, perhaps until late into the winter. They are an invitation to birds, squirrels, other animals, and to you and me to come and gather them and so distribute the seeds that are inside the fruits.

Most of us think of fruit as the juicy, flavorful foods we eat—apples, oranges, grapes, plums, strawberries, cherries. But what we usually think of as vegetables—beans, tomatoes, peppers, cucumbers— also are called fruits by the botanist. So are grains, like corn, wheat, and oats. When we want to be very exact, we say a fruit is a ripe ovary of a flower with its seed or seeds; the ovary is the enlarged lower part of the pistil that becomes the fruit.

Nature puts seeds in many different "packages" for several reasons. The packages protect the seeds. They help spread the seeds. They furnish food for people, animals, and birds. They help us tell one seed from the other. Seeds to be sold in stores are put in bright paper envelopes for like reasons—to attract us and let us know one kind of seed from another.

Botanists group and name the different types of fruits in several ways in order to describe them in a few exact words.

We may find it interesting to classify fruit in order to see the many kinds and types and to learn more about the ways in which they are formed.

We can put all fruits into three groups according to the number of ovaries—pistils—involved in forming them.

An *aggregate fruit* is formed by one flower that has many ovaries. Each of the separate ripe ovaries we call a "fruitlet." A strawberry is an example of this kind of fruit. The fruitlets are scattered over the surface of the red, fleshy part, the "fruit" that we eat. It is really the enlarged end of the flower stalk. The fruitlets are the tiny, dry, yellow things, which we speak of as seeds and which are so small we might overlook them. Raspberries and blackberries also are aggregate fruits.

Raspberry

Strawberry

A *multiple fruit* develops from the ovaries of many separate flowers, which are clustered closely together. An example is a fig in which many flowers grow inside a hollow container, which we eat. It is a flower stalk that has become thick and sweet. The outside is smooth, and you do not see the seeds, but if you cut it open you see a mass of small seed-like fruits within the fleshy stalk. Or when you eat a fig, you can feel in your mouth the small, hard seeds. The mulberry and pineapple are other examples of multiple fruits.

Nearly all common fruits, except the ones we have named, are simple fruits.

A *simple fruit* consists of a single ripe ovary. There are many kinds—the grape, cucumber, orange, plum, apple, bean, sunflower, corn, maple, carrot, and nut. But, you say, they are all so different! An orange doesn't look at all like a kernel of corn! Nobody can say a tomato is the same as a peanut! All those simple fruits are alike in that a single ovary produces them, but they are different in firmness (or fleshiness), in form (or structure), and in the way they open when they are ripe. Each of the fruits mentioned in this paragraph is an example of a different type of simple fruit.

We divide simple fruits into two main kinds— fleshy fruits and dry fruits. Each of those two kinds is in turn divided into various groups, but we do not need to name them all.

Of all the fleshy fruits, you may know the apple best. Pears and quinces are much like an apple in

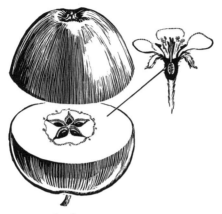

Apple

form and also are known as pome fruits, or apple fruits. The part of the apple that we eat is a part of the flower, which has grown thick and fleshy. The seeds themselves are in five thin, papery cells of the core.

Tomato   Grape

49

Berries also are fleshy fruits. They are pulpy all the way through. Very likely you have eaten gooseberries, currants, and cranberries. Maybe you have never known that grapes and tomatoes also are classified as berries. Oranges, grapefruit, and lemons are berries that happen to have a thick, leathery rind. A date is a berry with one seed. The ovary that produces a date has three parts; after pollination, one part enlarges and makes the seed, and the other two parts disappear. Squashes, pumpkins, melons, cucumbers, cantaloupes, and gourds are called gourd fruits. They really are a type of berry with a harder rind, or outside covering.

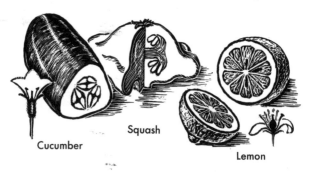

Cucumber

Squash

Lemon

The stone fruits, sometimes called drupes, are fleshy fruits also. They have an outer part that is fleshy or pulpy like a berry, but the inner part—the stone—is hard like a nut. Perhaps you have thought the pit or stone of a peach is the seed, but

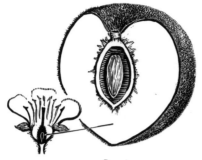
Peach

it is not. It is really part of the "fruit." Crack the peach stone open and you will find the seed itself, and you will see that it has its own seed coats. The same is true of olives, almonds, cherries, apricots, and plums.

The dry fruits—the second big class of simple fruits—ripen without pulp or flesh. These are of several kinds. They also are divided into two main groups—those that split open when they are ripe and those that do not split open.

The most common and most interesting of those dry fruits are the pods, which split, and grains, key fruits, and nuts, three of the dry fruits that do not split open.

The pod fruits are legumes. Legumes are very important in agriculture—next in importance to members of the grass family—because they are the only class of plants which can increase nitrogen

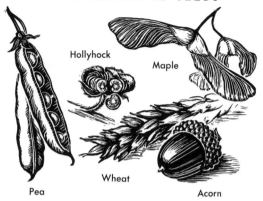

Hollyhock

Maple

Wheat

Pea

Acorn

of the soil and because some of them are good forage plants. Among the legumes are peas, peanuts, beans, vetch, alfalfa, and clovers; some trees, like acacia and honey locust; and sweet peas and lupines, which are lovely plants for flower gardens. You are most familiar with peas and beans. They are in pods when we pick them off the plants in the garden. The peas and beans that we eat have been taken out of the pods. They are the seeds. Peanuts, despite their name, are more like peas than nuts. The unshelled peanut is a pod. The part of the peanut we eat is the seed inside the dry pod which we crack open. The thin, brown, papery covering of the peanut seed is the seed coat. The pods of peas and peanuts split easily and can be split open lengthwise.

Nuts have hard shells and contain only one seed.

The walls of the seeds become hard and do not split open of themselves—we have to crack them open if we want to get the nut-meats out. Examples of nuts are acorns, chestnuts, and hazelnuts. Acorns are the fruit of oak trees and come in little cups. It is interesting to know that some things that we usually think of as nuts are not nuts at all—at least according to the definition we have of nuts. The part of the walnut you eat is the seed itself. It has been removed from its shell, perhaps before you bought it at the store. Before it reached the store, though, the shell that enclosed the nut had to be removed from a green or dark-brown husk or hull in which it grew. Thus, strictly speaking, the walnut is really a stone fruit (or drupe), because its shell corresponds to the inner part of the ovary wall; the outer part is fleshy. The same is true of the almond; it also grows inside a hull, which we remove.

Grain is the dry, small fruit of plants of the grass family. Wheat, corn, rice, barley, oats, and rye are examples. Each dry fruit (which we call a grain) has one seed.

Most plants produce fruits only if there is pollination and fertilization and if seeds are produced. That, as you remember, means that pollen from the stamen reaches the pistil—the ovary—and then quickens it into life. But some plants can produce fruits without those steps. Among them are certain kinds of eggplants, navel oranges, some kinds of peas and apples, a kind of cucumber, and the banana. Gardeners recently have learned how to grow tomatoes without seeds and with more "meat" by spraying the blossom with certain chemicals.

It is interesting to be able to tell the names of wildflowers, trees, and some other plants by their seeds and fruits in the fall and winter after their flowers and leaves are gone.

Here are some you might like to know:

Jack-in-the-pulpit: Many bright red berries cover a stubby club that once was the "jack." Indians used to boil the berries and eat them.

Wild groundcherry: A five-sided brown husk encloses a reddish berry, which can be eaten.

Alder: Black, conelike fruits.

Mountain-ash: Handsome clusters of bright red fruits, which look like tiny apples.

Buckthorn: Black, rounded, berrylike fruits, each with two to four seeds.

Creeping wintergreen: Bright red, spicy, mealy fruits, like berries, that ripen in October.

Dwarf cornel, or bunchberry: Round, red berries in tight clusters, that are carried aloft on a stem after the flowers fade in June and July. Dwarf cornels grow in deep, rich woods.

Bittersweet: An orange-yellow capsule, like a berry, which splits open when it is ripe and curls back to show the scarlet coating of the seeds.

Dwarf wake-robin: A reddish berry in three parts and about one-half inch thick.

False Solomon's seal, or wild spikenard: A cluster of red, speckled berries, which have a spicy smell.

Twisted-stalk: A red berry that has many seeds.

True Solomon's seal: A blue-black berry.

Sumac: Dense clusters of fruits, which may be red, orange, whitish and hairy—depending on the variety.

Pokeweed: Juicy, purplish berries that begin to ripen in August and hang in long clusters on red stems.

Sumac   Bittersweet   Jack-in-the-pulpit

5 : TO CLOTHE THE EARTH

One day in August of the year 1883 two volcanoes erupted on Krakatoa, a small tropical island between Java and Sumatra in the East Indies.

The explosions lasted all day. They could be heard a thousand miles away. They blew into the air a mass of rock and pumice six miles wide, six miles long, and six miles deep. The explosions destroyed all of the island except one mountain peak, and that was covered with a thick layer of smoking ashes from deep inside the earth. Trees, shrubs, small plants, and animals were wiped out. A French botanist who visited Krakatoa nine months later found there only one sign of plant or animal life—

a lone spider, which was busily spinning a web. All else was barren, lifeless, and seemingly unable to support any kind of living thing.

The closest island, twelve miles away, also was covered with hot ashes. The ashes and poisonous gases from the volcanoes killed the plants on that island. Twenty-five miles of ocean separated what was left of Krakatoa and the nearest untouched land.

But three years later a Dutch botanist visited Krakatoa and found many seashore plants growing near the beach. Farther inland he discovered ferns and grasses. Ten years later other scientists found the island well clothed with beefwood trees, orchids, coconut trees, and wild sugar cane.

How did the plants get across the twenty-five miles of ocean to that barren island?

Wind carried the fern spores, the very tiny, seed-like bodies which grow into fern plants, although they are much smaller than seeds. Even gentle air currents can carry spores and small seeds great distances. Wind also brought the orchid seeds, only slightly bigger than spores, and some of the smaller grass seeds to the island.

But the coconut seeds were too big to be transported by wind. Coconut palms grow along the

shores of tropical islands in the Pacific and Indian
Oceans and the seeds that drop from them may be
carried away by the ocean waves. They can float
for several weeks in sea water, protected by their
thick husks and hard seed coats. Some washed
ashore on Krakatoa, where they were moistened by
fresh water and sprouted. Coconuts sprout without
being covered with soil.

Birds also must have carried some seeds to Krakatoa, maybe those of papaya and fig trees.

Men who came much later brought with them
some fruit trees, but those trees did not live very
long before the growing jungle crowded them out.

The story of the reclothing of Krakatoa is more
than a story. It is a lesson in one of the main points
of natural history, which is the story of Nature. Let
us go a little more deeply into that story.

Seeds when they are ripe have to be brought in
some way or another to places where they can
grow. It would not do for the seeds merely to drop
to the ground near the mother plant. Soon there
would not be room in that small space for them
to grow. Think of what would happen if all the
kernels of all the corn cobs in a field of corn or all
the seeds from the trees in a forest just fell to the
ground. Most of the seeds would not sprout at all for

want of room. Many of them would not be covered. Many would be carried away by animals or water. The seeds that sprouted would be weak and would soon die because they would not be able to get food and sunlight.

Nature wants each kind of plant to live and continue to bear seeds, even though sometimes she does not seem to care very much about what happens to an individual plant.

That is one reason, for example, why she packed starch around the germ of the corn kernel. The starch nourishes the embryo as it sprouts. Man has found the starch to be a good food for himself and for animals, too, and therefore he stores, transports, and plants the corn so that he will have it when he needs it. Thereby—although he does not always think of it in that way—man helps Nature disperse the seeds over the world.

The four main carriers of seeds are birds, wind, water, and people, all of which brought seeds to Krakatoa. There are two other ways in which seeds are spread. One is by animals. The other is by a remarkable device that some plants have for shooting their seeds some distance away from the mother plant.

All over the world birds distribute many seeds.

Sparrows, blackbirds, larks, quail, doves, horned larks, and pheasants are among the birds that like seeds of weeds as part of their food. When birds digest the seeds entirely, the seeds will not grow, of course, and so the birds play a part in helping us get rid of weeds. But if the seeds are not digested, they pass out of the birds' bodies and begin to sprout where they are dropped. Thus the birds may spread unwanted weeds to grain fields and pastures.

Robins, bluebirds, catbirds, thrashers, thrushes, mockingbirds, crows, waxwings, and several other kinds of birds eat many kinds of fleshy fruits. They digest the soft pulp around the seeds. The hard seeds pass through their bodies unharmed or sometimes in even better condition for germination.

Sometimes the birds die with seeds inside their bodies. It often happens that the seeds then germinate. That is another way in which birds help spread seeds.

Some birds, such as the grosbeaks, finches, and crossbills, dig seeds out of pine cones. The seeds they eat are entirely digested, but the birds pry loose other seeds from the cones. Those seeds drop to the ground or fly away on their own little "wings."

Jays, crows, nuthatches, woodpeckers, and titmice

—and also squirrels and pack rats—often carry nuts, acorns, and large seeds away to store them. They may later forget about these hoards of food or they may die before they eat them. If so, the seeds are left to sprout in a place away from the parent plant.

Or, sometimes, seeds stick to the feet, legs, or feathers of birds and so get a long ride. Ducks and geese may have floating seeds on their feathers when they rise from the water and walk or fly to another place.

Crows are especially good seed carriers, because there are so many of them, they range over a wide area, and they gather in roosts with large numbers of other crows. One half of the diet of crows may be fruits of wild plants. The crows digest the pulp but expel the seeds, many of which may sprout under the places where they roost.

Birds seem to like especially well the cones, which resemble fleshy berries, of the red cedar tree. Robins, bluebirds, starlings, and about fifty other kinds of birds relish these fruits. The cedar waxwing, or cedarbird, in fact, gets its name from its fondness for the red cedar "berries." More than half of the red cedar seeds are spread by birds. Often the seeds are dropped at the fences where the birds perch. So they plant the seeds, and that is why you sometimes see a row of cedar trees along a fence. For the same reason you are apt to see Virginia creeper, wild grape, poison ivy, moonseed, bittersweet, dewberries, and other vines and shrubs which have fruits that birds enjoy, along fence rows and stone walls. The birds perched there and dropped the seeds after they had eaten the fruits.

So birds help us by planting forests and spreading seeds of vines, brambles, shrubs, and so on. Of course, not all the seeds are of plants that we want in our yards or fields. Among them may be poison sumac or poison ivy, but we have to take the bad with the good.

You and your dog very likely are good seed carriers when you walk in the country in the fall and, when you return home, pick off from your trousers and stockings or the dog's hair the needles, barbs, ticks, and burs that stuck to your clothes or the dog.

You do not like the burs and "stickers." If they touch your skin, they itch and prickle. They are hard to get out of the dog's coat. They are even worse if they cling to the wool of passing sheep, for they may mat the wool and have to be cut out. They may harm cows, horses, and other grazing animals when they stick to the mouth or throat, where they can cause sores that keep the animal from eating.

But even if they are unpleasant or harmful, Nature was very clever in making some seeds with barbs and hooks so as to be sure that they would be carried a distance from the place they developed. They are, indeed, wonderfully strange devices, as you will agree when you look at them with a magnifying glass or see them in a large drawing.

Take, for example, the cocklebur, which may grow in corn fields, wastelands, or on banks of streams. Its bur, a fruit, has spiny hairs that make it stick to anything soft. And here is a strange detail: A cocklebur has two seeds inside it. The half that contains one of them is soft, so that that seed can easily sprout the following spring. The other half is tougher and the seed is protected in it for a year or more. Thus cockleburs have a better chance of surviving than some other plants. Nature sometimes does not like to put all her seeds in one kind of basket.

Burdocks are another pesky plant that has barbed seed cases. They do not like cultivated fields; they prefer rich places around farm buildings or pastures. Each bur contains many seeds. Farm boys like to throw the burs at each other. But burs are not fun to animals. A traveler who visited Chile years ago said he saw horses with manes so full of burs that they could hardly walk. Now, of course, much of the land in our country and other countries is farmed so carefully that there are fewer of these

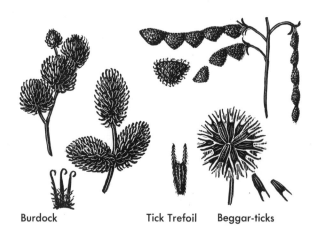

Burdock   Tick Trefoil   Beggar-ticks

pesky weeds. Farmers do everything they can to get rid of them by cultivating and by using chemicals that kill weeds.

Some weeds have seed cases with thorns, claws, and spines as sharp as needles. An example is the South African grapple plant, which has a dozen sharp claws. Wild animals and farm animals can easily step on them. The claws are forced into the feet or the cleft of the hoof and cause great pain and sores. Even lions have gotten claws of the grapple plant into their mouths and have starved to death because the claws kept them from eating.

Cowboys know and dread a plant they call devil's claws, or devil's horns. Its pretty flowers develop into long, sharply hooked pods, or shells, that remind you of pincers. They seem to grab hold of the leg of a horse, sheep, or cow and dig deeper and tighter into the flesh when the animal tries to get rid of them. The animals go almost crazy with pain and have severe sores if the claws are not removed.

Farmers in England rubbed their eyes in wonder at the strange plants that were coming up one summer in a neighbor's fields. They counted twenty kinds of weeds they had never seen before. Finally they found the reason. The neighbor had used as a sort of fertilizer on his fields some waste wool from mills in Yorkshire. The wool had come from Australia. In it were burs and weed seeds that had got tangled in the sheep's coats. They had to be cleaned out before the wool was spun into cloth. They were in the waste that the farmer had put on his field, and they soon sprouted. That was a long journey for the seeds—but that is not all. Most of the plants that produced the seeds were not Australian natives. They had been brought to Australia from their original homes in North America, Chile, and the Mediterranean countries.

So, when you pick stickers out of your dog's coat after a walk or run in the fields, you may be sowing a new crop of weeds if you just throw them on the ground. You are most apt to find these weed seeds:

Beggar-ticks, which have two prongs that point outward.

Spanish needles, which are long and slender and have four curved prongs.

Pitchforks, which are short and broad and have four prongs. They are the fruit of the bur marigold, which grows in swampy soil.

Sandburs are round, spiny, and one-fourth inch across. They have sharp hooks.

Bedstraw has hooked bristles on the plant. The fruits are spiny or sometimes smooth.

Stickseed has four nutlets from each flower. It grows in dry pastures and waste places. The nutlets break off the plant when you brush against it and are hard to remove from clothing or dogs.

Now we come to another of the main ways in which seeds are carried—water.

Rain and running water spread many seeds. Rivulets that run off sloping fields after storms, irrigation channels, floods, sewers, wind-blown rain in thundershowers, and water flowing in streets after rains are such good agents of seed dispersal that Nature might have planned them—but of course did not!—with that aim in view.

Many fruits and seeds are lighter than water and can float easily. Other fruits are made with a sort of envelope or sack that contains air and helps them to float. Sometimes water carries seed only a few feet. Sometimes our large rivers carry seeds from one end of the continent almost to the other.

Wind is another of Nature's helpers.

We think of airplanes and gliders as marvelous inventions, and indeed they are. But think of the ways seeds have of flying—and have had for countless ages!

Sycamore   Ash, Elm, Maple   Dandelion

Some air-borne fruits are called winged fruits. They have enlarged wings or margins. Seeds of maple, elm, and ash are examples.

The name "parachute fruits" is given to those—such as dandelion, lettuce, and many of the thistles—that have spreading tufts of hairs, or scales, or bristles at one end. The tiny, dry, light parachutes are lifted from the plant by wind or by a person or lawn mower or something else, and float far away. All of us, I suppose, have picked a dandelion when it has gone to seed and have tried to see with how many puffs of breath we could blow away the whole mass of tufted seeds.

Groundcherry and hop hornbeam are examples of plants whose fruits are in paperlike cases or sacs that have air in them, somewhat like small balloons,

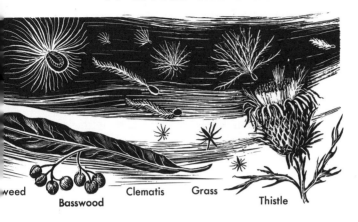

weed   Basswood   Clematis   Grass   Thistle

to help them move in the wind.

Among the most interesting of all the fruits are the key fruits. We do not eat them, but sometimes we play with them. Elm, ash, and ailanthus (tree of heaven), maple, and box elder trees have key fruits, or keys. Some keys contain one seed. Some, like those of the maple, have two seeds. The keys are thin, oval wings which help the seeds fly over a wide area, and remind us of airplane propellers. Maybe you have put one of the wings, like tissue paper, between your thumbs and whistled through it, or sailed the maple keys through the air, to see how far they will go. The wings are an outgrowth of the wall of the pistil. If you take away the wing or wings, and remove the outside covering, you will see the seed inside. Ash trees sometimes produce

69

large bunches of winged fruits, which hang from the branches after the leaves have fallen.

Seeds of milkweed, willow, and cotton have long, silky hairs, which enable them to fly. (Cattails do, too, but a cattail technically is a fruit, not a seed.) Clematis and anemone have dry fruits with long plumes formed from the stalk and branches at the top of the pistil.

We mentioned airplanes and gliders. One plant has seeds that can glide as far as one-fourth of a mile, and they are studied by scientists who believe the seeds can tell us more about flying. Gliding and flying are much the same.

Those seeds were found some years ago in a jungle in Java. They grow on vines that can climb to the top of the tallest trees. The vines are sometimes called Zanonia, although that is not their right botanical name. They flower in January and February. The large fruits ripen, open, and drop the large seeds in August, when the winds there are mostly from the east. The seedlings almost always are found on the west side of the trees on which the vines grow. That shows that the seeds glide downward and not into the wind. The seeds have "butterfly" wings almost as thin as tissue paper and about six inches across. They sail like small

gliders until they strike a tree. The few seeds that happen to fall on open ground do not sprout. Because they need trees on which to climb, Nature made sure that they would not sprout in places without trees by making germination possible only in shady spots.

Engineers who study the principles of flight have discovered some interesting things about the Zanonia seeds. The seeds have a wing loading equal to about one-hundredth of a pound to a square foot of area. That is about the same as that of a butterfly's wing.

They studied the seed's center of gravity, which is the point in an object around which its weight is evenly balanced. The scientists learned that the seeds would glide farther and not so fast and steeply if the center of gravity was moved back from its front tip. How could the seeds glide at all without fins, which most airplanes have to steady them in flight? It was found that the weight of the seed at the center makes the tips bend upward, thus giving the seed the steadiness it needs.

Gliders have been built along the lines of the Zanonia seed, and the swept-back wings of the all-wing type of aircraft owe a lot to the lessons learned from the flight of the seeds.

People, of course, do more than wind, birds, water, and animals to disseminate seeds of cultivated plants and weeds. That is partly because seeds and fruits and other parts of plants are so important to us as food and as sources of other useful products.

Some seeds we plant in our gardens, fields, orchards, forests, and greenhouses because we want the food the plants yield. In fact, we can say our whole way of living was made more possible when our ancestors long ago discovered that they could save seed from the grain harvest in the summer or fall and plant it the next year for a steady supply of food.

People convey seeds all over the world in many ways, sometimes by accident, sometimes by intention. We do not need to name all the ways here—

72

but why don't you see how many ways you can list?

Two men who spread large amounts of seeds are especially interesting. Perhaps you have heard of Johnny Appleseed, an American pioneer and legend. His real name was John Chapman, and he was born in Massachusetts in 1774. He lived in Pennsylvania and he used to give or sell seeds and seedlings of apples to families that were moving westward to settle. In 1806 he started down the Ohio River with two canoes filled with apple seeds. When he came to a place that looked suitable, he would stop and plant an orchard. For forty years he wandered through Ohio, Illinois, and Indiana, helping settlers to plant and care for their apple trees. He did a great deal for the pioneers by giving them seed, and even today we speak the name of Johnny Appleseed with great respect.

Another man who, like Johnny Appleseed, has spread seeds far and wide is Aloysius Eugene Francis Patrick Mozier, a merchant seaman on an American freighter. He was a Marine in the Second World War, and in Korea he saw people suffering because they did not have enough good food, especially vegetables. He decided that he could help people by getting them seeds. So every time his ship returned to the United States he bought seeds of carrots, tomatoes, turnips, and other vegetables. When the ship docked in a foreign place like Pusan, Kobe, Calcutta, Bombay, or Inchon, he would set out to distribute the seeds. He has delivered more than a million packages of seeds in 1953, 1954, and 1955. On one trip he took two hundred fifty thousand packages.

Here is one more example of the way people have scattered seed.

Seed of the Russian thistle, one of the worst weeds farmers ever have had to cope with, first came into the United States from Europe in some flaxseed, which was sown in South Dakota in 1886. Within nine years the thistle had spread over sixteen states. Now it is a pest in much of the western part of the United States. The wind carries the whole plant in the fall when its seeds are ripe, and the plant tumbles along over many miles, scattering the seeds. The seeds—like seeds of many other weeds—can also be carried in hay, feeds, and sacks of crop seeds.

Pigweed, witch grass, and other weeds like them, which we call tumbleweeds, also are rolled along by the wind when they are dry. There are other thistles which have bunchy purple flowers, stiff, prickly leaves, and fluffy seeds that easily fly away in the breeze.

And now we come to the last of the ways we mentioned by which seeds are disseminated. (*Disseminate* means to scatter or spread, but your dictionary will tell you that it comes from two words: *dis,* which means in all directions, and *semen,* which means seed. Therefore *disseminate* has a special meaning—to scatter seed.) This way is a way some plants have of their own.

Some plants can shoot their seeds into the air when a drop of rain hits them with some force. One kind of evening primrose keeps its seed capsules closed when they are dry. The capsules open quickly and take on a cup shape when they are wet. Then, if a drop of water strikes them hard, the seeds are scattered quite far.

Violets have wedge-shaped seeds in pods. When the pod gets dry and shrinks, it bursts open and throws the seed several feet away from the parent plant.

The jewel weed, or touch-me-not, is a wildflower that you may see along roadsides. It has pretty yellow-orange and brown-spotted flowers with a long curved spur. When you touch the pod in which the seeds are, it shoots the seeds away as though it were a small gun.

Pansy and witch-hazel plants also shoot their seeds out of pods—not very far, but far enough to give them a better chance to grow.

6 : FOOD AND STRENGTH FOR ALL

People of different countries may give the name *corn* to their main grain crop. When Scotsmen speak of corn, they mean what we call oats. In England, corn means our wheat. In some translations of the Bible, corn is used to mean barley.

When we in the United States speak of corn, we mean Indian corn or maize or *Zea mays,* which is the scientific name.

There are several kinds of corn. We like to eat the white or golden sweet corn that we grow in our gardens or buy in cans or frozen packages. We all know popcorn. We feed to animals the kind that usually is called yellow dent, a truly noble plant that sometimes grows as tall as a small house and bears large ears of plump, rich kernels.

Yellow corn is one of the few native American grains. Most of our other grains have been brought here from other countries.

Corn is a member of the large and useful grass family. Wheat, barley, rye, oats, rice, sugar cane, and the true grasses are cousins (or perhaps we might say brothers and sisters) of corn. Botanists group them in one family because they are alike in the basic structure of their stems, leaves, flowers, and some other parts.

Corn was cultivated in the Americas long before the white man came. Two Spaniards from Christopher Columbus' crew in 1492 found in Cuba "a sort of grain they call maiz which was well tasted, bak'd, dry'd and made into flour." Columbus called it Indian corn.

But the corn we grow today had its origins much farther back than that. Maybe it took as much as twenty thousand years for our modern corn to develop. We do not know the plant from which it first came. It might have been a seed-bearing grass, *teosinte,* which grows wild in Mexico and Guatemala.

To the ancient Indians, corn was a sacred, God-given, priceless treasure. The Mayas, who lived in Central America hundreds of years ago, had a hero, Gucumatz, who traveled far, suffered many hardships, and nearly died to bring his people their greatest good—corn.

The Inca had a god of fertility, Manco-Ceapac, who brought corn to the people. The Inca thought of him as a wandering farmer with a stout staff, which he used to test the soil to see if corn would grow in it.

The Pima Indians believed in a goddess who lived alone and always came to them with corn when they were hungry.

The Indians said prayers and conducted feasts and ceremonies to thank the gods that gave them corn. They took their choicest seeds of corn with them when they moved to another place.

They early discovered an important fact. Corn seldom seeds itself, as other grains like wheat and rice can and do. The corn plant would drop its heavy ears at the foot of its stalk and there the kernels would lie, unable to spread themselves. The next year perhaps several kernels would sprout from the half-buried ear and produce a clump of small corn plants so thick that no ear would grow. It is sometimes said that the corn, if not attended by man, would die after three years, but that statement is not entirely correct. Corn plants occasionally grow wild. Rodents and other mammals sometimes disseminate the seed.

Corn has always been a mainstay in America. Colonists who came from England to Jamestown in 1607 soon learned that the seed they brought with them did poorly in the Virginia climate. Captain John Smith, their leader, found out about corn from the Indians and he ordered every colonist to grow an acre of corn. Thus the colony was saved from starvation.

The Pilgrims also had a hard struggle when they landed at Plymouth on a cold December day in 1620. Their food supplies were alarmingly low. When Miles Standish was returning empty-handed from a discouraging hunt for meat one day, he found baskets of corn buried in Indian mounds. He bought the corn from the Indians. The Indians showed the Plymouth colonists how to plant and cultivate corn so they could grow their own the next summer.

The pioneers who moved westward to settle the new frontiers of America carried seeds of corn with them as a prized possession. Corn was good food for themselves and their families and animals. Corn was easy to grow and highly productive in the prairies of the Midwest. More and more of it was grown.

It became the main crop in the Midwest.

Year after year the farmers chose their best ears of corn for planting the next year. Year after year they chose good plots of land for growing their corn, fertilized well when necessary, and tended the corn fields carefully. The corn plant thus has improved from year to year, generation to generation, and century to century.

In 1918, a war year when food of all kinds was badly needed everywhere, American farmers raised corn on 110 million acres of land, and harvested three billion bushels. In 1941-1944, when another war was being fought, American farmers again produced four tremendous crops of corn—three billion bushels each year. But corn was grown then on 89 million acres—eleven million fewer acres than in 1918. That is almost the same as saying that in those four years American farmers raised five crops of corn!

That great accomplishment was made possible by planting seed of hybrid corn.

Today the word "hybrid" is in common use. We speak of hybrid tea roses, hybrid zinnias, hybrid chestnuts, hybrid chickens, hybrid barley, and other hybrids. People sometimes use the word to describe any new kind of flower or vegetable that is bigger or stronger than the parent plants, or to mean something of mixed origin. But it is more accurate to say that a hybrid is the offspring of two plants (or animals) of different species or varieties. The offspring usually are bigger or stronger or otherwise better than the parents. That is called "hybrid vigor."

The development of hybrid corn began with the discoveries of an Austrian monk named Gregor Mendel. He studied peas to learn how definite traits, like tallness, were passed on from parent plants to offspring. He kept careful records of how often a particular trait appeared in the offspring of plants he grew and on which he himself placed just the pollen he wanted.

Gregor Mendel gave a speech before a club in his home town in 1865 and he told about his experiments. He published a report of his work in 1866. But his work was not appreciated until 1900. Then at last three scientists, working independently, rediscovered it and confirmed his findings. They were de Vries in Holland, Correns in Germany, and von Tschermak in Austria. Mendel's discoveries soon became the key that unlocked many doors.

George Harrison Shull opened one of the doors. He was one of six sons of a poor Ohio farmer. An older brother, too poor to go to school, taught himself botany and gave his books to George when George was twelve years old. From then on George devoted himself to the study of plants. He worked his way through school, college, and university, and he became director of a new experiment station at Cold Spring Harbor, New York. His task was to study the effect of heredity—the traits that plants and animals pass on to their offspring. He chose corn to study because it is important and because it can be grown quickly and easily.

On a small plot of ground he grew corn year after year. Each season he made tests. He measured the size of each plant. He counted the number of ears on the plants and the number of kernels on each ear. On some plants, before the ears formed, he made sure that only the pollen of one plant would fall on the "silk"—the threadlike tip of the pistil— of that same plant. That is called self-pollination. On other plants he would transfer the pollen of one plant to the "silk" of another. That is called cross-pollination. It is also called open pollination or wind pollination when it happens naturally, without any help from people.

Before long he made a startling discovery. The self-pollinated corn was producing many types, some of which were smaller and weaker than the corn he started with. But the corn plants he got when he put pollen from one self-pollinated parent on the "silk" of another self-pollinated parent were taller, more productive, and more uniform than the ordinary open-pollinated corn he started with.

So George Shull decided that the corn he started with, like the corn Indians and farmers had grown for years, really was hybrid corn, in which many types and traits had been mixed up by natural wind pollination. The ears looked alike, but were not. They were rather large because they had some hybrid vigor. The ears he got after careful self-pollination were smaller because they lacked that hybrid vigor, but they also had fewer mixed-up types. Therefore, he believed, by repeated self-pollination year after year he could get the exact trait he wanted —whether it was big ears, or uniform ears, or many

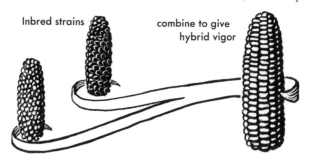

Inbred strains   combine to give hybrid vigor

ears, or taller plants. Then, when he had worked that part out, he believed he could cross-pollinate two of those plants and get hybrid vigor back again.

He grew seven generations of self-pollinated plants. Each year the ears were smaller than the ears he got the year before—but they were pure, unmixed strains with the traits he wanted.

Finally he placed the pollen from one of these seventh-generation plants on another seventh-generation plant. That is, he used cross-pollination again. The result was indeed startling. The seeds that resulted produced plants that in size, health, and uniformity were better than their parents and also much better than the plants he started with in the first place.

George Shull's work and ideas seem simple enough now, but at that time they were strange, unheard-of, and, to some people, foolish. Some farmers asked, "Why go to all that trouble and expense when a faster and easier way to improve corn is merely to choose the best ears each year, plant them, and let the wind do the pollinating?"

But George Shull and other plant breeders who worked with hybrid corn proved to be right. They gave us one of the greatest discoveries of all time.

Since then great strides have been made in breeding better corn. It is long and tedious work to produce such hybrids, for great care must be taken so that only the wanted pollen, from carefully selected father plants, reaches the seed-producing organs of the mother plants. Even so, it is easier to control pollination in corn than in many plants in which stamens and pistils are small and close together in the same flower. In corn, the flowers are male and female. The many male flowers, with stamens, form the tassel which can be cut off to prevent self-pollination. Female flowers, each with a pistil consisting of grain and long "silk" to receive the pollen, are crowded together to make an ear.

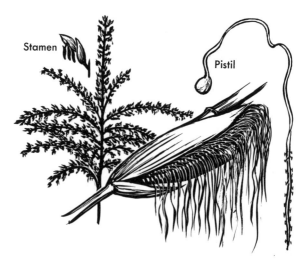

Hybrid corn is said to be twenty per cent better than corn that is naturally pollinated. The plants are stronger and are less easily blown down by storms. They withstand diseases better. The ears are more uniform and bigger. The kernels contain more food. That is, they have hybrid vigor.

Now nearly all farmers who grow corn plant hybrid seed. Hybrid corn is grown on about eighty to ninety million acres in the United States. Our corn crop in 1954 was about four billion bushels.

Corn also is grown in many other countries because it is good food for people and animals and has many uses.

The drawing, which shows the inside of a kernel much bigger than it really is, marks the parts of a kernel and the valuable things it is made of.

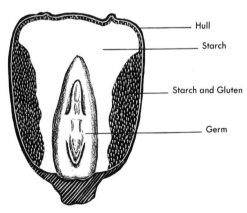

On the outside is the hull, the seed coat. Just under it is a thin layer mostly of gluten, which contains protein (*pro*-teen). Toward the center is a mass of starch and gluten. Near the top and around the germ is the white starch, which Nature put there to nourish the growing embryo. The germ—the embryo—contains oil and protein.

Nearly eight-tenths of the kernel is starch. About one-tenth is protein, which is a necessary part of the cells of plants and animals. The rest of the kernel is made up of oil, fiber, and minerals. All, but especially starch, are important as food for the growing seedling and for man and animals.

You are familiar with corn flakes, corn bread and muffins, corn chips, canned corn, and ear corn, which you eat as a vegetable.

Corn meal, flour, and grits are used in many ways for food. So is cornstarch—but did you know cornstarch is used in making chewing gum, tooth paste, mustard, table salt, soap, baked beans, and yeast?

Corn syrup, being sweet, is used in cookies, powdered coffee, condensed milk, jams, sausages, tobacco, vinegar, and many other products.

Manufacturers may use sugar from corn in making or processing doughnuts, pancake flour, cheese spreads, chocolate products, penicillin, salad dressing, and other foods and drugs.

Corn oil is used for cooking many things, like potato chips, and may be a part of margarine and mayonnaise.

Industries use one or another product from corn in an almost endless number of ways. Let us name a few of them: Asbestos, gypsum board, book bindings, cigarette sealing, chalk crayons, doll heads, envelopes (glue), fireworks, ink, matches, cold-water paints, paste, sandpaper, shoe polish, liquid soap, rayon, chemicals, airplane dope, safety glass, coated paper, stencil paper, and hats.

We can count more than five hundred uses for the corn plant and the products we get from the kernels.

And so we end our study of just one seed—but what a seed it is!

Corn, of course, is an outstanding plant, but many of the facts about it are true also of other seeds and plants. The more you read about them, the more you will understand and value the wonderful things of this wonderful world.

7 : WHEN YOU BUY SEEDS

The seeds you buy at a store—where did they come from? Who grew them?

Behind them is an interesting story, part of which you already know.

You know how flowers of plants produce seeds. You know that even plants that are closely related differ greatly. Sweet peas, as an example, may be pink, orange, crimson, maroon, blue, lavender, scarlet, white, purple, and cream-colored. Some may be tall and some short. Some may bloom early and some late. Some may be healthier than others.

You also know that certain traits are passed on from the parent plants to their offspring.

You read how we pick out and plant the seeds of some plants that we think are especially good. Natural selection is the term given to selection by Nature, when a plant better suited than another to a particular combination of sun, soil, and moisture survives and others die because they are not so well suited. Selection by man is much the same. Plants that are unusually strong or beautiful are chosen for improvement. Like the corn that we have just read about, they are cross-pollinated, or "crossed"— that is, the pollen from one chosen plant is placed by hand on another selected plant, so that the seed that results will produce a plant superior in growth, size, health, beauty, or some trait that we think is good.

Much of what we know about all this is based on the painstaking work of Gregor Mendel, to whom we have already been introduced.

Gregor Mendel was born in 1822. When he was twenty-one years old he entered a monastery at Brunn, Austria. There he started his experiments with peas. Very carefully he kept complete records of many plants from several generations. You could appreciate the amount of tedious work he did if you would plant a hundred pea seeds and when they got big you would list for every plant its exact height, the color of its flowers, the number of its leaves, and the shape of its seeds. And then the next year, and the next and the next, plant all the seeds you got from plants of a certain height—and then keep precise records of them. Most of us would not try to do it even for one year!

From his many experiments with peas, Gregor Mendel discovered some important facts about how plants (or, we can say, all living things) get certain qualities from their parents and their parents' parents, and so on.

He learned that one quality, such as tallness in peas, is inherited separately from other qualities. Some qualities, which we also call traits or characters, are stronger than others. That is, they are dominant. But other qualities also are carried from one generation to another, although they may not be apparent in all the plants. Those characters are called recessive. So, if plants that are bred for several generations to be tall are crossed with plants that are bred to be short, the dominant character— in this case tallness—will be seen about three times as often in the offspring as the recessive, the weaker character.

Gregor Mendel studied pairs of characters to see which one of the two traits would appear oftenest.

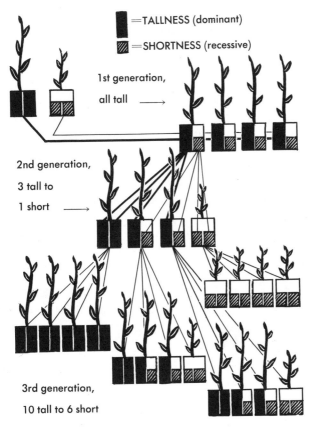

=TALLNESS (dominant)

=SHORTNESS (recessive)

1st generation, all tall ⟶

2nd generation, 3 tall to 1 short ⟶

3rd generation, 10 tall to 6 short

Roundness and wrinkles in the pea seeds, tallness and dwarfness, and purple and white in the flowers were some of the pairs of characters he studied. When the plants that have the particular traits are crossed, one of the two characters is dominant and the other becomes recessive, but which is which can be found out only by repeated tests. Tests have shown that roundness is dominant over wrinkledness, tallness is dominant over dwarfness, purple is dominant over white.

At first many people scoffed at or overlooked the obscure monk's discoveries, but finally they were accepted for what they really were—a tool that has made it possible to develop bigger, better, healthier, or more beautiful plants.

And now let us look further into the development of peas—only this time it is the sweet pea, the sweet-smelling, lovely flower that gardeners love so well. It is very much like the white flower of the garden pea, but larger and of many colors. Like the garden pea, the sweet pea likes cool weather. That is why gardeners in the warmer parts of our country have had trouble in growing sweet peas.

That brings us to the work of Frank G. Cuthbertson, who is vice president of the Ferry-Morse Seed Company and its director of seed breeding. His work and his company are examples of the work of many plant breeders and firms in many countries.

Frank Cuthbertson was born in Scotland, where his father was a director of a seed company. Frank began working there as soon as he finished school.

But he wanted to come to the United States, and in 1911, when he was twenty-four years old, he sold his bicycle, shotgun, and other belongings to help pay for his steamship ticket to America.

He went to California, got a job with a seed company, and ever since has devoted himself to the breeding of plants.

He rose rapidly in the firm. Soon he was put in charge of all of its work of breeding better kinds of vegetables. He knew that many fine varieties were to be had, but he believed that every one could be improved, no matter how good it was.

Mr. Cuthbertson and the men who worked with him improved a long list of vegetables that surpassed previous kinds in at least one respect. That is, they found the desirable character that they wanted and bred those plants until the character was "fixed"—that is, it appeared in all later generations.

One was a beet. Beets sometimes are attacked by mildew, a disease. So the plant breeders found beet plants that seemed to be able to resist mildew better than others. Seeds of the healthier plants were planted one year. Of the healthiest ones of those, seeds were selected and planted. And so on, year after year, until the factor that carried the greatest resistance to the disease was firmly fixed in all later generations. And at the same time other desirable factors showed up, one at a time—a nice, regular shape and a deep red color all the way through. The variety was given the name of Resistant Detroit Dark Red Beet.

Another was a cantaloupe with a new and useful quality. Powdery mildew is a disease that can be prevented by applying sulfur to the plants, but ordinary cantaloupes die if sulfur is put on them. So Mr. Cuthbertson developed a cantaloupe on which sulfur can be used to prevent powdery mildew.

We could name many more—a carrot that is orange-red and tender clear through the core; hardy cabbages that resist yellows, a common disease of a number of vegetables; a cucumber that commercial growers prize because it always averages eight inches long. In all, Mr. Cuthbertson and his team of scientists have given us six improved varieties of beans, three of beet, five of broccoli, six of cabbage, three of cantaloupe, five of carrot, ten of cauliflower, six of celery, one of sweet corn, three of lettuce, two of parsley, two of parsnip, five of peas, two of pepper, seven of tomato, and one each of radish and squash.

They also worked to improve zinnias, pansies, larkspurs, marigolds, petunias, and other flowers.

One spring day in 1931 Mr. Cuthbertson was checking some sweet pea seedlings in his company's trial grounds in Salinas, California.

He noted one seedling that was different from the others. Its flowers had a poor, dull blue color, but the vines of the plant were very strong and its flower stems were unusually long.

He saved the seed from that husky plant and planted all of them. He again saved and planted the seed of the strongest. He did so a second year. Then he felt sure that the strong growth and long stems were outstanding characters that could be bred true in all later generations.

But the dull blue flower color was a poor char-

97

acter, and he set about getting rid of that. He crossed them with another strain in which earliness of bloom, size of blossoms, and clear colors were fixed characters.

For ten years he continued that work of crossing, testing, and selecting the best of each generation. Finally he was satisfied that the new type would be the same year after year in color, size, and earliness. Earliness was important, for that meant that gardeners in the warmer climates could now plant sweet peas. They are called the Cuthbertson sweet peas, and to the ones of different colors he gave the names of his family. Tommy is blue. David is bright rose crimson. Lois is rose pink. Evelyn is salmon pink. Coline is scarlet. Janet is white. One carries his own name, Frank G. It is lavender.

When all that was done, the task of growing enough seed for sale throughout the United States was begun. And now in many stores you can buy, for just a few pennies, packets of seed of these lovely flowers—a small price for all that work and care and beauty!

Mr. Cuthbertson's firm has big farms near Rochester, Michigan, and Salinas and San Juan Bautista, California, where men carry on the work of breeding, testing, and growing seed. That seed is planted on nearly thirty thousand acres in order to produce the seed that is sold to gardeners all over the world.

But that is not all of the work. More than thirty-five thousand tests are made every year to make sure that the seeds will germinate properly. More than thirteen thousand trials are conducted to prove that the plants are up to the expected purity of strain. Thousands of individual plants, which seem to have some unusual character of size or vigor or beauty, are enclosed in cages or bags to guard against unwanted pollination and watched closely. Their seed is planted separately so that the next generation can show whether the unusual character actually is there and is worth keeping. So the search for perfection goes on year after year.

Careful records are kept of every lot of seed—where it came from, how it was produced, and how it grew. The weak and inferior plants and seeds are destroyed. Only the best are kept and used to produce new crops of seeds.

Maps are made of every plot of ground in the stations where seed is produced. The location of beehives in the neighborhood is checked so that the chance of unwanted pollination by bees may be avoided.

The plant breeders have before them always a

picture of the ideal for which they are working. Books are kept with photographs, measurements, descriptions, and paintings of the perfect flower and the perfect vegetable of each variety, and that is what the scientists are trying to achieve. To see how close they are getting to the goal, the men talk with people who have bought and planted the seed. They go to canneries and freezing plants to inspect the vegetables being prepared there for canning or freezing. They go to markets and look over the incoming shipments of vegetables. They see the crops growing in the fields, to make sure they are all they should be and to learn whether more can be done to make them better.

All that you buy when you buy a package of good seed.

8 : WHEN YOU PLANT SEEDS

Half the fun of knowing about seeds is in planting them and watching them grow.

First, you must get the seeds, and that also is fun.

Some you will want to buy from a store or from a seedsman or dealer who sends out catalogs or advertises in the gardening magazines. The seeds you buy from them will be fresh, and of the kind they are supposed to be. The marigolds that grew this summer in your garden were pretty, but the ones you grow from their seed might not be quite the same or quite so nice.

Many people think it is great fun to go through the seed catalogs in late winter or early spring and make plans and dream about the garden that is to be planted when the ground is ready for the seed.

Or you might enjoy looking over the colorful display of seed packets in a rack at the grocery, hardware, or five-and-ten-cent store.

You won't have to wait until the outdoor planting time comes. You can start an indoor garden on a window sill in winter.

Get some strong paper drinking cups. Better still are jelly glasses or peanut butter jars, for through the glass you will be able to see how the roots develop. Fill them three-fourths full with garden soil or soil mixed half-and-half with sand. Nasturtiums, zinnias, morning-glories, peas, beans, and gourds are fine for planting in the cups. If you plant morning-glories, you should soak the seeds in water for twenty-four hours to soften the seed coats and then nick them with a file or knife before planting them. Put two or three seeds in a cup. Cover them with soil to the depth that the instructions on each package say you should. Then, after you have planted your "garden," fill each cup with as much water as it will hold without running over.

Now here are some rules that you should follow for the sake of the plants and for the sake of yourself and your mother, who wants to keep things neat. Put some strips of newspaper on the window sill first, in case you spill some water even though you water very carefully. Fill the cups with soil in the basement, on the porch, or in the kitchen, putting down old newspapers before you begin. If you should spill any dirt, sweep it up. When you have planted the seeds, leave them alone. Do not try to see if they are sprouting. Put water in the cups only once a day. Do not water too much; you might "drown" the seeds. But if you see that the soil in the cups seems to be getting very dry between waterings, you may have to water them twice a day or three times in two days.

Now comes about two weeks of waiting for the first tiny seedlings to come up. Be patient.

If you would like to see how the seeds sprout in the soil, press a few nasturtium seeds down in a jelly glass right next to the glass, where you can see them. Water carefully. In a few days you will see the seed putting forth new life.

You may want to plant some seeds indoors so that you will have plants to put in your garden outside as soon as warm weather comes. Many gardeners do that in February or March, and thus get a head start on spring. This is more ambitious than the window-sill garden and it takes more equipment. You can do it, though, without too much trouble or expense if you are careful.

You will need a shallow wooden box (which is called a "flat" and is about two feet wide, three feet long, and three inches deep), or a cigar box, or a metal or plastic pan in which to plant the seed. Even old coffee cans will do. Some gardeners use soil or sand that has been heated in the oven so as to kill the fungus that causes the damping-off disease of seedlings. Much better are vermiculite or shredded sphagnum moss, which you can buy at stores that sell garden supplies. You plant the seed (it may be nasturtium, zinnia, bachelor's-button, marigold, for example) not very deep in the box or pan, firm down the soil with a brick or a board, water the soil well, and keep it covered with newspapers or a pane of glass (to keep too much of the moisture from evaporating) until the seedlings are up. When they have put out their true leaves, you plant them in soil in a pot or can until the right time for planting them in the ground.

You can easily get more information about the time for starting seeds indoors, how to plant and care for them, and materials to use. Some seed catalogs, garden pages of newspapers and magazines, gardening magazines, radio and television programs, and books give the information. Very handy plant-starting kits, which include some waterproof boxes for starting the seeds, larger boxes for the seedlings, and even packages of seeds, are advertised. I think you will enjoy using them. You may find this a most rewarding hobby.

If you have never had a garden before or if you know of nobody from whom you can get advice or help if you need it, it may be best to start with rather large seeds, which are easy to handle and plant. (Not that gardening is hard or takes a lot of knowledge and experience! It takes some patience, some work, and some loving care and understanding.)

Very likely it will be best to start with some of these flower seeds: Nasturtium, zinnia, pot marigold (or calendula), cornflower (or bachelor's-button), cosmos, California poppy, four o'clock, coneflower, toadflax, and marigold. You can transplant the young plants to your outdoor garden when the ground warms up. That would be in April or May, depending on which part of the country you live in.

All of these are hardy annuals—that is, they grow and produce seed in one season and then die. (Perennials live year after year, even though the leaves and stems die down in the fall.) Hardy an-

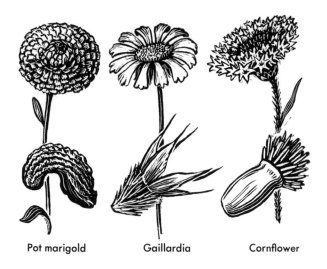

Pot marigold   Gaillardia   Cornflower

nuals stand some frost in the spring and can be sown in the garden where they are to bloom.

The packages the seeds come in have information printed on them about height, time of blooming, their color, the ease with which they are grown, and some details about planting.

Some vegetable seeds you might like to plant in your garden are lettuce, parsnips, turnips, Swiss chard, green beans, carrots, beets, peas, and radish.

Gourds are fun to grow if you have a large garden and a fence or sturdy trellis the vines can climb on.

This is not a book about gardening, so I suggest that you write a postcard to the Office of Information, United States Department of Agriculture, Washington 25, D. C., for a useful booklet. Just write: "Please send me a free copy of *Growing Vegetables in Towns and Cities, bulletin G7.*" The booklet, which has illustrations, will give in detail the information you need.

Here are a few suggestions about planting.

Choose a sunny place for your garden.

Spade or plow the soil well, and before you plant seeds, smooth the ground well. Mark the rows with string or twine so they will be straight.

Sow the seed as deeply as the directions on the package tell you. Be careful not to plant them too deeply.

The time of sowing depends on the variety of the plants and the part of the country you live in, but generally you can plant hardy annuals about a month before you expect the last frost.

Water the plants if there is little rain.

Seeds must have the right combination of water, air, and warmth if they are to germinate.

Seeds absorb more water in warm weather than in cold weather, and so the seed coats will soften more quickly in late spring. That does not mean that the warmer it is the better seeds will sprout.

We can say that most seeds need a temperature

of about 60 to 70 degrees to germinate, but some seeds like lower temperatures and some sprout best at higher temperatures.

Men in seed-testing laboratories have made many tests to find out the best temperatures for the germination of seeds. They have found that radish, lettuce, peas, barley, and wheat will germinate when the temperature is as low as 39 to 60 degrees. Seeds of corn, pumpkin, cotton and many other plants need 69 to 80 degrees. A gardener or farmer does not have to go out with a thermometer to measure exactly how warm the ground is when he wants to plant seeds, but he has to know in a general way which seeds will need quite warm weather in order to sprout. Otherwise the seeds may just rot in the ground and not grow.

It will not do to plant some heat-loving plants like corn and tomatoes before the ground is warm in late spring or early summer. They are tender and freeze easily. Some other plants, like peas, want cool weather, and must be planted as early as the ground can be spaded and made ready.

Sometimes gardeners use a process they call stratification (strat-ih-fi-*kay*-shun) to get seeds of trees and shrubs to sprout. It is simply a way of keeping the seed moist and cold for a while. It is, so to speak, using Nature's way of letting seeds sleep under the snow or frozen leaves through the winter. It helps soften the hard seed coats and often makes the food in the seed ready for the embryo. Perhaps you would like to try it as an experiment with seeds of dogwood, holly, or barberry, which should not be too hard to get.

All you need for stratification is a glass jar or tin can, some cheesecloth, and peat.

In the piece of cloth, about eight inches by ten inches in size, wrap the seeds. Roll the cloth up tightly and put a rubber band around it. Place the roll in the jar and fill it with damp peat or sand.

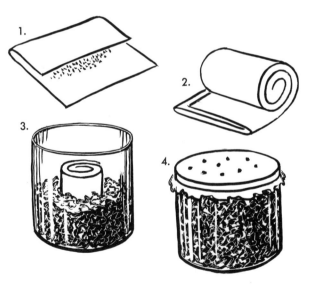

Over it put a cover of waxed paper in which you punch holes for air. Put it in the refrigerator.

About once a month, unroll the gauze or cheese-cloth and look at the seeds. Some seeds start to swell and split in three or four weeks. Others take three or four months. If you see no signs of germination, put the jar back in the refrigerator for a few more weeks. Make sure that the peat or sand is damp.

When the seeds start to swell or split, plant them in a shallow tray. Fill the tray with a mixture of equal parts of sand, loamy topsoil, and peat. Water with a fine spray and provide some heat from below—perhaps by placing on a radiator. Keep the tray covered with a folded newspaper until the seeds sprout. Then remove the paper. When the seedlings have two sets of true leaves, carefully transplant them into a seed flat or can in which you have put a mixture of sand, loam, and peat.

You might also like to try stratification for sprouting wildflowers, like Virginia bluebells.

You can collect wildflower seeds in the fall and save them until planting time. Many of our wildflowers are disappearing from our woods and countryside, and everybody who can should try to save them.

If you find any of them, or buy wildflower seeds

from dealers who collect and sell them, plant them in a woodlot, giving them much the same care you would give seeds in your garden.

With wildflowers our exploration of seeds and their ways comes full circle. Of all the plants that clothe the earth and have been put to use by man, the wildflowers have survived the struggle for existence without much help from us and against many obstacles. They show in their own quiet way the urge to live that is in every seed.

INDEX